Poems for Loners

Douglas Richardson

Also by Douglas Richardson

The Corruption of Zachary R.
Weak Creature Press 2009

Out in the Cold, Cold Day
Weak Creature Press 2009

Sugar Fish
The Sacred Beverage Press 2007

Poems for Loners

Douglas Richardson

Weak Creature Press
Los Angeles

Poems for Loners
©2010 by Douglas Richardson
Weak Creature Press
First Printing, August 2010

All rights reserved. No part of this book may be used or reproduced in any manner whatsoever without written permission from the author except in the case of brief quotations embodied in critical articles or reviews.

This is a work of poetry and fiction. Any resemblance to actual persons, living or deceased, events, or locations is entirely coincidental.

Library of Congress Control Number: 2010933106
ISBN: 978-0-9842424-2-9

Printed in the United States of America.

Cover design by Heather DeSerio, Precision Edge Design LLC.

Joshua tree photo by Douglas Richardson.

Author photo by Jen Cairns.

For information on other publications available from Weak Creature Press, please email weakcreature@aol.com.

Contents

Author's Note

Introduction

Poems and Lyrics

Proverbs

Notes from the Graveyard Shift

Notes from the Grand Canyon

Twenty Days of Isolation

Barney Murdoch

Bald Family Man

Human Beings, for Example

Museum Diary

Index

Acknowledgments

About the Author

Author's Note

Poems for Loners blends poetry and storytelling. The book has nine distinct parts with interwoven plots and themes that progress from beginning to end. The parts are scattered more or less evenly throughout the book, like pieces of a puzzle. An index is available should the reader wish to revisit any specific part in its entirety.

-Douglas Richardson

Introduction

Poems for Loners is fearless in both content and convention. Skillfully managing both poetry and storytelling, as the author's note states, Douglas Richardson traverses the landscape of human anguish, offering an exceptional and luminous portrait of subjectivity.

Richardson's archetypal loner is no sad sack that dines on bitterness, self-pity, and alienation; instead, this tragic hero—cast in various personas—pursues human flaw, embracing the inevitability of despair, regret, longing, *and* hope with profound wryness and piercingly authentic, if not brilliantly twisted, grace.

Pieces written in first person and omniscient points of view intermingle with recurring settings, a nifty schema that underscores themes of yearning and searching. From the gray hollow of the graveyard shift, the bright sun of the dry Arizona desert, to the Los Angeles and London museums that map the collection, *Poems for Loners* is a hauntingly beautiful walkabout.

-Tess. Lotta, editor of *Media Cake eMagazine*, poet, and writer of *Perjurious Strumpet* blog.

For Jen

1.
When loner was born
he didn't know how to speak,
just like this afternoon
when he woke from a long nap.

2.
Wind and sea
become fog
over the land
and
through the trees
of my dreams.

3.
Julia is gone.
She left for the ancient forest and will not return.
She said someone wants to do her harm.
She said someone wants to do her wrong.
Julia is gone.
Now I think about her all the time.

4.
Notes from the Graveyard Shift:
We sit silently at our stations waiting for work.
There is time to think.
There is time to listen for answers.
We fear what might happen
if we lose our jobs: insomnia, starvation,
the violence on the streets during these hours
which, for us, are hazy and placid.
The halls in our building are dark.
The lights turn off for lack of motion.
There is time to think.
There is time to listen for answers.
We hear the ticking of our watches,
the hum of the air vent.
We think, If death is like the graveyard shift,
that wouldn't be so bad.

5.
Notes from the Grand Canyon:
I walk west along the tracks
at the south rim of the Grand Canyon.
Faint vibrations have become a steady rumble.
I refuse to turn and look
in a perverse test of faith.
I wedge my feet under the rails
and brace for impact.
Nothing, except for grease on my sneakers.
I turn around.
There's that Indian again.

6.
On the first day of isolation
loner chose not to go home;
on the second day of isolation
loner denied he was alone.

7.
Dear Mrs. Smith:
I understand that you process my monthly payment on behalf of the General Motors payment processing center in Phoenix, Arizona. I understand that you have processed car payments for 23 years. I understand that a serial killer is shooting the citizens of your city and that your husband was gunned down by this serial killer at a self-serve car wash. Enclosed please find this month's payment. I cannot comprehend the magnitude of your loss, but hope this letter eases your grief. Also, please understand that I am available to read any correspondence you wish to send my way. You may send it to my home address in Los Angeles, which is the billing address reflected in your records.
Sincerely,
Barney Murdoch

8.
Peace on earth and goodwill within,
said the bald family man.
Speak freely with the opposite sex.
Have two children.
Watch your two children cross the street
with thirty other children,
hands joined, single file.

9.
Every month or so, loner remembers
two translucent kids from the neighborhood
who died in a plane crash when loner was seven.
When he thinks of them he says,
I will never forget you.
It's the other way around, they say.

10.
One white balloon
in one blue sky
on one green lawn
my body does lie.

11.
Don't make fun of Tara.
Her eyes are distant yet intense.
She addresses everyone by first and last name.
She once wore the most beautiful dress
I have ever seen.

12.
There was no dress.
There were thread and fabric.
There was no Tara.
There were memory and mystery.

13.
If asked,
I would say the color of a gull is
white, gray, pewter: a reflection
of the sea.
If asked,
I would say the color of the sea is
blue.

14.
At 5,000 feet,
loner sees tiny creatures battling over
pretty patterns of land.
At 5,000 miles,
loner sees a masterpiece of
color and light.

15.
Notes from the Graveyard Shift:
Because you are human beings, for example,
you expect vivid descriptions of the character
quirks of we who sit silently at our stations
waiting for work.
We are reluctant to indulge you, however,
because we are skeptical of such descriptions.
We find they are mostly exaggerations and
are sometimes outright lies.
There is nothing phonier than a big personality.
There is nothing more demeaning
than a nickname.
Work with us for a month and you will
appreciate our position on this matter.

16.
Notes from the Grand Canyon:
The hotel is in a remote area
between the south rim and Flagstaff.
It is run by Indians.
My heart feels warm and safe until I realize
I am the only guest.
At 3 a.m. I hear snoring not my own.

17.
On the third day of isolation
loner survived by eavesdropping
on gossips and louts;
on the fourth day of isolation
loner survived by tuning them out.

18.
Dear Building Super:
I have a leaky shower
and a leaky sink
and there's a screw loose
in my doorjamb.
Warm regards,
Barney Murdoch

19.
Peace on earth and goodwill within,
said the bald family man.
Drink your wine,
it is almost summer.
Read your book,
the light is bright.

20.
Because you are human beings, for example,
you read poems for loners on cold Sundays.
You put off brushing your teeth,
however,
until bedtime,
which lessens your enjoyment of the reading.

21.
Monday I watched the day disappear
outside my window
napped on and off with my shoes on
didn't go outside because the museum was closed.

22.
Photographs, postcards, and spider guts
decorate the walls of loner's room.
He watches DVD movies on an old color TV.
He reads many books and magazines but
rarely finishes any of them.
An unabridged dictionary is his preferred surface
for eating and writing.

23.
Loner's hope is revived through freeway culture.
Speed through the future. A river flows.
Alone in the car. A cloud captivates.
Turn the radio dial.
Find a song that suits the cloud.

24.
Julia heard a song by the loner who scared her.
The song was too intense,
the way his voice cared for her.
Julia is gone, sang loner.
Julia is gone.
She left for the ancient forest and will not return.
She turned off the radio,
but his voice still haunted her.

25.
Trains arrive and trains depart,
either way it breaks my heart.

26.
Too much cleverness
extinguishes the light in the left eye;
too much sarcasm
the light in the right.

27.
Ocean is the opposite of cancer.
Star is the cure for space.

28.
Notes from the Graveyard Shift:
There isn't much difference
between night and day.
Both are lit by stars,
as any space traveler knows.

29.
Notes from the Grand Canyon:
At 9 a.m. I buy moccasins
in the hotel souvenir shop.
My sneakers are permanently stained.
I eat breakfast in the hotel café.
The Indians do not smile.
They make me feel right at home.

30.
On the fifth day of isolation
loner wrapped himself in a shroud;
on the sixth day of isolation
loner sought refuge in a crowd.

31.
Dear Mrs. Smith:
Thank you to you and General Motors for processing my early final payoff check in the amount of $2,482.23. I was reluctant to send this early payoff because I felt a certain affection for our monthly transaction, which had become a source of pride for me, a former welfare recipient on the verge of bankruptcy. Also, please note that I am in receipt of the overpayment refund check in the amount of $0.44 from your Knoxville office. I will promptly deposit this check which, despite its nominal sum, further demonstrates your integrity. It has been a pleasure working with you toward ownership of my vehicle.
Hosanna,
Barney Murdoch

32.
The busboy pushes his cart past my table.
Noisy dishes.
Noisy families.
I long for the sound of waterfalls.
I long for the next trance.

33.
Tea bag twirls above my cup.
Tea streams into tea.
Sanity at last.

34.
The only way to achieve peace on earth is to blow up the moon.

35.
Because I'm a human being, for example,
I linger in gray sky cathedrals.
Original prayer is rare,
but the lines in my face
are more valuable anyway.
Season after season after
season after season
the lines in my face will deepen.

36.
Apostles pass through my fever
sweat on my temples
mouth agape for maximum air.
I lie on a sidewalk lined with eucalyptus.
Crosses, gargoyles, and ice
line the Catholic church across the street.
I want to be Catholic.
I want to believe the Apostles.
I want to love this fever.

37.
Stoic as I wanna be
got a schizoid personality
I'm so lonesome – go away.
Stoic as I wanna be
got a whiskey right in front of me.
I go psycho when I'm drunk.

38.
Loner spends post-blackout mornings
filling cracks in the sidewalk,
thinking Dear Prudence.

39.
Notes from the Graveyard Shift:
Lunch hour is at 3 a.m.
We always take lunch in the lunchroom because
we are afraid to leave the building at this hour.
If we take a disagreeable bite,
we are free to spit it into the lunchroom sink
without fear of judgment or reprisal.
We are also free to genuflect and to pray out loud.
When lunch hour is over,
we wash our dishes in silence.

40.
Notes from the Grand Canyon:
After breakfast I get into my car.
I drive east along the south rim
and into Navajo country.
The moccasins feel slick on the accelerator,
on the brake pedal.
I buy a pipe in the shape of an eagle.
I touch frost in the mouth of a cave,
though the temperature outside is 90 degrees.
I hike a volcano to see a crater.
There's that Indian again.

41.
On the seventh day of isolation
loner felt threatened and bought himself a gun;
on the eighth day of isolation
loner hid himself away from the sun.

42.
Dear Mrs. Smith:
Your loss still burdens my mind. So much so, that I am neglecting the basics of food and water, sleep and hygiene. I have been drinking bourbon and writing and tearing up letters to you. I have been driving for miles in the open desert. I have lost all sense of responsibility, but I don't seem to care.
Yours,
Barney Murdoch

43.
Peace on earth and goodwill within,
said the bald family man.
Don't buy bourbon for the crazies
under the freeway.
They'll tear you to pieces
when one of them dies drunk.

44.
Loner brings daisies to the crazies
under the freeway.
Lives are saved,
but the mood doesn't change much.

45.
Peace on earth and goodwill within,
said the bald family man.
Bring pennies to the crazies under the freeway.
Listen to them scream.
The sound becomes pure like a choir
and they fly away.

46.
Tuesday I went to the Tate Modern in London.
One room had a wall with rain painted on it.
Then I understood how rain falls
vertically and horizontally simultaneously.
I took out a sheet of paper
and drew this effect myself.
I saw England with new eyes.

47.
Lord have mercy on my soul
I'm very sad
and very dull.

48.
Loner hears words that wound.
Loner becomes killer.
Loner hears words that heal.
Loner becomes savior.

49.
I'm still a little baby
and I want you to love me.

50.
The bottle of dish soap I've had
for five years is finally empty.
I'm afraid I've grown attached to it,
but it would be crazy not to throw it away
and get a new bottle.
I know what I'll do.
I'll buy same brand, same size, same color.
No. I'll wander off and never come back.
Hosanna.

51.
Julia read a letter from the loner who scared her.
The letter made no demands
but still caused great fear in her.
It wasn't cute or playful,
the way he cared for her.
She packed her belongings and
arranged for her departure.

52.
Loner went down to the water
to exorcise demons from a harlot
and other illusions
only to discover later
that he didn't need to go to such extremes
to get a girlfriend.

53.
There is famine in a foreign country.
My stomach is full.
I don't have to fight for food in my country.
I love the sound of wind in palm trees.

54.
Notes from the Graveyard Shift:
Preparations for work begin just after sunset.
When the sky has darkened, we prepare our
lunches and then sit as still as possible
to conserve energy.
Listening to classical music is advised.
Reading is not.
You may be surprised to learn that few of us
think of ourselves as night owls and that
most of us are connoisseurs of sunrises,
rather than moon phases.

55.
Notes from the Grand Canyon:
Night arrives. I decide not to stay another night in the Indian hotel. Instead, I check into an EconoLodge in Flagstaff. I unpack my clothes. I set the pipe in the shape of an eagle on top of the TV. I go into town for dinner. Breathing is difficult this high above sea level. Every tenth breath is a gasp. I find a bar & grill. I sit at the bar. The bartender is friendly. The woman next to me is not. She makes fun of my skin, which has turned red in the sun. Every fifth breath is a gasp.

56.
On the ninth day of isolation
loner lost his vacated home;
on the tenth day of isolation
loner called himself alone.

57.
Dear Building Super:
Never mind the noises coming from my apartment. They are nothing more than the usual sounds of obsession and compulsion: papers tearing, bottles opening, and whatnot. Thank you for repairing my shower, sink, and doorjamb.
Warm regards,
Barney Murdoch

58.
In this part of time be gentle.
Then comes pain.
In the next part of time, be gentle still.

59.
Life on earth is dying again.
Come visit me in my childhood home.
In time there will be air again.
In time fish will be reborn in the sea.
But this does not concern me now.
Come visit me in my childhood home.

60.
Because I'm a human being, for example,
I enjoy a fragrant bouquet of balloons.
I also enjoy the scent of a tire shop
and a bicycle shop.
I enjoy the smell of rubber,
gasoline too.

61.
Peace on earth and goodwill within,
said the bald family man.
Be grateful for your wheelchair;
it is a tool for better living.
Be kind to your war veteran;
you, too, are a killer.

62.
The autumn sun was gentle as a folk song
as the soldier passed by my table,
steam rising from my teacup
warm and gray as a
Confederate widow.

63.
Notes from the Graveyard Shift:
We are known to see faces in the clouds.
We came late to the facts of life.
In fact, we must maintain a list
or we lose our way.
The list usually goes something like this:
What is a fact?
A fact is not a theory.
A fact is reality.
The facts of life are God,
Love, Death,
Hunger, Thirst,
Sex.
Sometimes when we see faces in the clouds,
we cross Death off the list.

64.
Gazing out his office window
one rainy day, loner thinks:
What does my computer have to do
with those clouds?

65.
Notes from the Grand Canyon:
Back in my room in the EconoLodge,
I examine my red skin in the blank TV screen.
I take a hit from the pipe in the shape of an eagle.
The effect is like frost in the cave of my mouth.
Breathing is no longer difficult
this high above sea level.
At 3 a.m. I hear snoring not my own.

66.
On the eleventh day of isolation
loner packed his gun in the trunk of his car;
on the twelfth day of isolation
loner drove off to find Julia,
who couldn't have gone far.

67.
Dear Mr. Murdoch:
My name is Ms. Catherine Davenport. I work in the mailroom at the General Motors payment processing center in Phoenix, Arizona. I am responsible for processing undeliverable mail. You may be surprised to learn that no one by the name of Mrs. Smith works here, and as a consequence, your letters found their way to me. While it is quite possible you have a screw loose, I am nevertheless pleased to inform you that your letters achieved a positive result. Two women here in the Phoenix office did indeed lose their husbands to the serial killer you wrote of in your first letter. Both of these women were despondent without their husbands. I took a chance and showed your letters to Mrs. Harvey and Mrs. Peterson and I am happy to report that both women found comfort in your words. All of us here in the Phoenix GM payment processing center are deeply touched by your humanity. Best wishes to you, and congratulations on owning your GM vehicle.
Sincerely,
Catherine Davenport

68.
Wednesday I began at the
Arc de Triomphe in Paris.
I rode the elevator, called l'ascenseur, to the top.
I looked down the Champs-Élysées and
I heard a girl say, La Grande Roue, which is the
Ferris Wheel with the giant AIDS ribbon.
I ended at the Louvre viewing paintings by
Delacroix, of the cross.

69.
Loner went to the aquarium
and secretly cried
when he saw a frowning fish.

70.
Because I'm a human being, for example,
I enjoy aiming for 19 on the dartboard.
It's exactly where it should be,
on the bottom, to the left of 3.
I often get a triple score, which is 57.
It's hard to picture where the other
numbers are, except for 20,
which is at the top.

71.
Loner is haunted by Latin,
by the pathos of the living past:
Ego tibi memet relinquo, mihi veniam da.
I abandon myself to you, have mercy.
Praeclarus inersque somniare maneo.
Noble and inert, I dream on.

72.
Dark orange flower
in the late afternoon,
what is your name?
I didn't notice you this morning.
I was watching prams pass by
on this path through your garden.
Dark orange flower,
the days are growing longer
for our delight.
Still, no one looks our way.
They smile at the babies instead.

73.
Quit now
hear the girls giggle
the bees buzz for others
O loner
always on the verge of dying.

74.
Olive oil is evidence that the sun loves the soil.
Sunflower is evidence that the soil is grateful.

75.
Notes from the Graveyard Shift:
(4:15 a.m.)
The moths are awake at this hour, orbiting a desk lamp. They don't believe in night prowlers, incubi, or succubi. Nor do we. This shift can make a realist out of anybody.
(4:45 a.m.)
Where did the moths go? Who turned off the lamp? What was that chill? Those shadows? Who slammed the door? Oh, we must have nodded off. Hosanna.

76.
Notes from the Grand Canyon:
At 4 a.m. I decide to investigate
the source of the snoring.
I open the hotel door, which leads into a cave.
I walk through the cave,
which opens onto the shore of the Colorado River
in the depths of the Grand Canyon.
There's that Indian again,
his snores echoing against the canyon walls.

77.
On the thirteenth day of isolation
loner drove through the desert and ran out of gas;
on the fourteenth day of isolation
loner set off on foot toward a mountain pass.

78.
To Whom It May Concern:
When I was strong I wrote a series of letters that saved the lives of despondent widows in Phoenix, Arizona. Now I am weak and need your help. My loneliness has intensified my interest in you. I own a car and am willing to travel any distance to meet you.
Lamentations,
Barney Murdoch

79.
Peace on earth and goodwill within,
said the bald family man.
If you are a bachelor go often to the Laundromat.
Sing along with the oldies.
Handle your clothes with care.
Soon you will have a wife and son
to keep you company.

80.
Loner likes his girlfriend best
when she is asleep.

81.
The living don't receive enough credit;
the dead are given more than their due.

82.
Because I'm a human being, for example,
I will always fear death.
My gratitude increases with each orbit of the sun,
but I am no less afraid.
There's just no getting used to it.

83.
The tallest tower is a glorious achievement,
but it stirs up the winds below.

84.
Some beards are easygoing, with nits.
Other beards hold hateful edicts.

85.
Notes from the Graveyard Shift:
On bad nights, we work like satellites,
like drifters in the dark periphery.
On bad nights, we know not to answer voices that
ask, Where is your girlfriend sleeping tonight?
It is better to occupy ourselves with Internet
articles, such as "Hubble Reveals Ghostly Ring of
Dark Matter" or "Mars Experiment Might Help
Earthling Insomniacs."

86.
Notes from the Grand Canyon:
The colors of the canyon walls awaken at dawn
and the snoring subsides.
The Indian rubs his eyes and says,
Your skin has turned red like the canyon walls.
I offer him a hit off the pipe
in the shape of an eagle.
He breathes the smoke deep into his lungs
and leads me to a canoe on the riverbank.

87.
On the fifteenth day of isolation
loner hiked the mountain pass
into the ancient forest;
on the sixteenth day of isolation
loner collected amethyst.

88.
Thursday I was cloistered
at the Getty in Los Angeles.
This museum is a monastery atop a hill.
This museum is a flight dream
made of Roman stone.
I took the Appian Way to the sea.

89.
Dear Mr. Murdoch:
You will be pleased to learn that your letter To Whom It May Concern, which you posted in the Phoenix Sun and in certain coffee houses, has found my eyes. I understand your loneliness and, although your methods are unusual, they are not without charm. How long were you in the Phoenix area? Do you plan to move here? I need to meet you. My number is listed. Please call as soon as you read this. There is still time, but who knows how much.
Love,
Catherine Davenport

90.
Peace on earth and goodwill within,
said the bald family man.
Don't die if you're a loner;
a new friend will come if you stick around.
You will find a wife who completes your solitude,
who speaks to the plants
when your ear's to the ground.

91.
Being bad comprises sugar, paranoia, insomnia.
Being good comprises floss, trust, sleep.
Being good is more rebellious than being bad
because it disobeys instinct.

92.
A person who says I love Halloween
believes she is being rebellious.
It is more rebellious if that person says
I hate Halloween.

93.
Whenever loner receives a kiss,
centuries of kisses flash before his eyes.
Awkward loners with melancholy eyes
and fear in their bellies, lashing out for affection.
Whenever loner receives a kiss,
it is difficult for him to maintain his composure.

94.
When loner spent time with the first girlfriend of
his life, he said it felt like the afterlife.

95.
Notes from the Graveyard Shift:
We who sit silently at our stations
waiting for work understand immediately when
one of our own is in trouble.
Just last week one of our security guards began to
obsess on the *Texas Chainsaw Massacre*.
The rest of us called a meeting in the halls,
which caused the lights to turn on,
which gave us an idea for an intervention.
We requested, and our security guard agreed to
three days of intensive light therapy without
sleep. We are happy to report that he now
watches surf movies.

96.
Notes from the Grand Canyon:
I board the canoe and the Indian pushes it
off the riverbank and into the river.
From the shore the Indian says,
How strange that I see you everywhere I go.
I nod and wave to him as the canoe
moves west with the current.
See you again soon, I reply.
The Indian laughs and walks off along the shore
in the opposite direction.

97.
Because you are a river, for example,
you move away from your source
and toward your destination.

98.
On the seventeenth day of isolation
loner saw Julia by a stream in the sun;
on the eighteenth day of isolation
loner was glad he forgot his gun.

99.
Dear Building Super:
Here is my room key.
Here is my gun.
I'm off to meet Catherine
in the valley of the sun.
Warm regards,
Barney Murdoch

100.
Peace on earth and goodwill within,
said the bald family man.
Listen to your wife describe the
twists and turns of her day.
They are as perilous as the
curves of her body.

101.
Because I'm a human being, for example,
I feel great compassion for others when I see them
all small and nondescript on distant hills.
When others come closer, however, and I can
distinguish voices and personal characteristics, a
lifetime of harsh judgment descends and I retreat.

102.
Not too much righteousness
is best in church.
Not too much sin
is best in prison.

103.
Notes from the Graveyard Shift:
When the final graveyard shift ended
and we all went under,
we were delighted to discover
more than silent slumber.

104.
Notes from the Graveyard Shift:
We who sat silently at our stations
waiting for work see each other
in daylight in the outside world.
We see each other at beaches
or on park benches in the sun.
We can be spotted all around the world.
A liquid presence surrounds us,
as if we are swimming.
Outsiders catch themselves staring at us.
A curious peace overcomes them.

105.
Notes from the Grand Canyon:
Loner and Indian are not alone,
and the pipe in the shape of an eagle has flown.

106.
Friday I am cloistered at the Getty again.
I am troubled by the past and
never want to leave this sanctuary.

107.
On the nineteenth day of isolation
loner gave Julia an amethyst
as they lay in a clearing;
on the twentieth day of isolation
Julia said, Not all loners are worth fearing.

108.
Barney and Catherine are now together, proving the merit of love via letter.

109.
Peace on earth and goodwill within,
said the bald family man.
Don't mock my sincere advice,
though it may be quaint.
Don't judge my thinning locks,
or mistake me for a saint.

110.
Because I'm a human being, for example,
I'm cloudsick,
so look to the sky and love me.
I want to love you
like someone who doesn't exist.

111.
Like fireflies in the night
I wish you well.

Index

Poems and Lyrics: 1-3, 9-14, 22-25, 32, 33, 36-38, 44, 47, 49-53, 59, 62, 64, 69, 71-73, 80, 93, 94, 111.

Proverbs: 26, 27, 34, 48, 58, 74, 81, 83, 84, 91, 92, 97, 102.

Notes from the Graveyard Shift: 4, 15, 28, 39, 54, 63, 75, 85, 95, 103, 104.

Notes from the Grand Canyon: 5, 16, 29, 40, 55, 65, 76, 86, 96, 105.

Twenty Days of Isolation: 6, 17, 30, 41, 56, 66, 77, 87, 98, 107.

Barney Murdoch: 7, 18, 31, 42, 57, 67, 78, 89, 99, 108.

Bald Family Man: 8, 19, 43, 45, 61, 79, 90, 100, 109.

Human Beings, for Example: 15, 20, 35, 60, 70, 82, 97, 101, 110.

Museum Diary: 21, 46, 68, 88, 106.

Acknowledgments

Special thanks to my editors, Laura A. Lionello and Greg Dalgleish, for their expert guidance in the evolution and completion of this book.

Thanks also to *Poetry Super Highway* and *Media Cake eMagazine* for publishing individual poems from this book.

About the Author

Douglas Richardson was born on February 20, 1967, in Duluth, Minnesota, and was raised in Camarillo, California. He currently lives in Los Angeles, where he works as a proofreader, editor, novelist, and poet.

www.ingramcontent.com/pod-product-compliance
Lightning Source LLC
Chambersburg PA
CBHW020015050426
42450CB00005B/489